"INVESTING FOR EVERYONE: A BEGINNER'S GUIDE TO MUTUAL FUNDS"

MR. SOURABH D THAKUR

"This book is dedicated to all the individuals striving for financial freedom—those who dare to dream beyond limitations and take control of their financial future. To the beginners taking their first steps in investing, the seasoned investors refining their strategies, and everyone in between—may this book empower you with the knowledge to grow and prosper."

"A special thanks to my princess, my wife and my family, friends, and mentors who have inspired and supported me throughout this journey. Your encouragement and belief in my work have been invaluable."

— Sourabh D. Thakur

Contents

Foreword

Investing is often seen as a complex and intimidating subject, but in reality, it is one of the most powerful tools for achieving financial freedom. Mutual funds, in particular, provide an accessible way for individuals to grow their wealth, whether they are beginners or seasoned investors.

In today's fast-paced world, financial literacy is more important than ever. Many people earn money but struggle to manage and multiply it. That's where this book comes in—a comprehensive, beginner-friendly guide that breaks down mutual fund investing into simple, actionable steps.

Mr. Sourabh D. Thakur has crafted a book that not only explains the fundamentals of mutual funds but also includes real-life case studies and lessons from Rich Dad Poor Dad to help readers develop the right financial mindset. From choosing the right mutual fund to understanding market risks and maximizing returns, this book serves as a roadmap to smart investing.

Whether you're a young professional starting your investment journey, a middle-aged individual planning for financial stability, or someone approaching retirement, this book has something valuable for you.

I highly recommend this book to anyone looking to take control of their financial future and harness the power of mutual funds. With the right knowledge and discipline, anyone can achieve financial success.

Happy investing!

Preface

The journey to financial independence begins with knowledge. Yet, many individuals struggle to find clear, reliable, and easy-to-understand information about investing. Mutual funds have emerged as one of the most popular investment options, offering both simplicity and diversification, but for many, the world of mutual funds remains complex and overwhelming.

This book was written with one goal in mind—to demystify mutual fund investing and make it accessible to everyone, regardless of their financial background. Whether you are a beginner looking to start investing or an experienced investor seeking to refine your strategy, this book provides a step-by-step guide to understanding, selecting, and managing mutual funds effectively.

What Makes This Book Unique?

Unlike traditional investment books filled with jargon, this book follows a practical, reader-friendly approach. It not only explains the fundamentals of mutual funds but also incorporates real-life case studies and insights from Rich Dad Poor Dad to help readers develop a winning investor mindset.

Each chapter is structured to provide:
✓ A deep understanding of mutual fund types and strategies
✓ Guidance on choosing the right fund based on age and risk appetite
✓ Step-by-step methods to maximize returns and avoid common mistakes

✔ *Insights into market trends, behavioral finance, and long-term wealth creation*

A Note to the Reader

Investing is not about chasing quick profits—it's about long-term financial growth. This book encourages a disciplined and informed approach, empowering readers to take control of their financial future.

I sincerely hope this book helps you on your journey toward financial success and independence. Let's make your money work for you!

Happy Investing!

— Sourabh D. Thakur

Acknowledgements

Writing this book has been a journey of learning, exploration, and dedication. It would not have been possible without the support and encouragement of many individuals who have contributed in various ways.

First and foremost, I would like to express my heartfelt gratitude to my family for their unwavering support, patience, and encouragement throughout this process. Your belief in me has been my greatest motivation.

A special thanks to my mentors and friends, whose insights, guidance, and constructive feedback have played a crucial role in shaping the content of this book. Your expertise and wisdom have helped me refine my thoughts and deliver valuable knowledge to readers.

I would also like to extend my appreciation to the countless investors, financial experts, and authors whose work and experiences have inspired this book. The lessons from Rich Dad Poor Dad and real-life case studies included in these pages have been instrumental in making complex financial concepts easier to understand.

To my readers, thank you for trusting this book as your guide to mutual fund investing. Your passion for learning and taking control of your financial future is what truly drives this work. I hope this book empowers you to make informed investment decisions and achieve your financial goals.

Lastly, I would like to acknowledge everyone who has contributed, directly or indirectly, to the completion of this book. Your support has been invaluable, and I am truly grateful.

— Sourabh D. Thakur

Prologue

Money is a tool—one that can either work for you or keep you trapped in a cycle of financial uncertainty. The difference lies in how well you understand and manage it.

For decades, people have searched for the best ways to grow their wealth, yet many still struggle with where to invest, how to manage risks, and how to secure their financial future. Mutual funds offer an incredible opportunity for both beginners and seasoned investors to build wealth in a systematic, diversified, and professional manner.

This book is more than just a guide to mutual funds—it is a roadmap to financial independence. Inspired by the wisdom of Rich Dad Poor Dad and real-life case studies, it goes beyond technical knowledge and explores the mindset, discipline, and strategies that separate successful investors from those who struggle.

We live in an era where information is abundant, yet financial literacy remains low. The purpose of this book is to bridge that gap—to simplify investing, break down common myths, and empower readers to make smart financial decisions. Whether you are just starting or looking to optimize your investment strategy, this book will give you the tools and insights needed to navigate the world of mutual funds with confidence.

The journey to financial success starts with a single step. Let this book be your guide.— Sourabh D. Thakur

ONE

INTRODUCTION TO MUTUAL FUNDS – HISTORY, IMPORTANCE, AND EVOLUTION

1.1 What Are Mutual Funds?

A **mutual fund** is a professionally managed investment fund that pools money from multiple investors to invest in stocks, bonds, and other assets. Instead of buying individual stocks, investors purchase mutual fund units, gaining exposure to a diversified portfolio.

1.2 Why Mutual Funds?

Mutual funds are popular because they offer:
Diversification – Spreads risk across multiple investments.
Professional Management – Managed by experienced fund managers.
Liquidity – Easy to buy and sell at Net Asset Value (NAV).

Affordability – *Allows small investments through* ***Systematic Investment Plans (SIPs).***

1.3 How Mutual Funds Work

1.

   Investors pool their money into a fund.

2.

   The fund manager invests in different assets based on the fund's objective.

3.

   Returns are distributed based on each investor's share.

1.4 History and Evolution of Mutual Funds

The concept of pooling money for investment dates back to **1774 in the Netherlands,** *but modern mutual funds began in* **1924 in the U.S..** *In India, mutual funds started with the launch of* **Unit Trust of India (UTI) in 1963** *and have since evolved into a multi-trillion-dollar industry.*

1.5 Rich Dad Poor Dad Lesson: The Power of Passive Income

In Rich Dad Poor Dad, Robert Kiyosaki emphasizes the importance of making money work for you instead of working for money. Mutual funds help achieve this by allowing investors to earn compounded returns over time without actively managing stocks.

Example:

Suppose you invest ₹5,000 per month in a mutual fund with a 12% annual return.In 20 years, your investment would grow to ₹50+ lakhs, thanks to compounding!

1.6 Common Myths About Mutual Funds

Myth: *Mutual funds are only for experts.*
Fact: *They are designed for beginners too!*

Myth: *High returns are guaranteed.*
Fact: *Returns vary with market conditions.*

TWO

TYPES OF MUTUAL FUNDS – EQUITY, DEBT, HYBRID, INDEX, ETFS, ETC.

*Mutual funds come in various types based on their **investment objectives, risk levels, and structure.** Understanding these types helps investors choose the best fund based on their financial goals.*

2.1 Classification Based on Asset Class

1. Equity Mutual Funds (High Risk, High Return)

*These funds invest primarily in **stocks**, offering **high growth potential** but with higher risk. Suitable for **long-term investors** who can withstand market fluctuations.*

Types of Equity Funds:
Large-Cap Funds – *Invest in top 100 companies (e.g., TCS, Infosys, HDFC). Stable but moderate growth.*
Mid-Cap Funds – *Invest in 101-250th ranked companies (e.g., Tata Elxsi, Trent). More growth but riskier.*
Small-Cap Funds – *Invest in companies ranked 251+ (e.g., Happiest Minds, Deepak Nitrite). High growth but very volatile.*
Multi-Cap Funds – *Invest across large, mid, and small caps for balanced risk & return.*
Thematic & Sectoral Funds – *Focus on specific sectors (Technology, Pharma, Banking). Higher risk due to concentration.*

2. Debt Mutual Funds (Low Risk, Stable Returns)

These funds invest in government bonds, corporate bonds, and treasury bills. Suitable for conservative investors looking for stability.

Types of Debt Funds:
Liquid Funds – *Ideal for parking short-term cash. Low risk, returns around* **4-6%***.*
Short-Term & Ultra Short-Term Funds – *Good for 1-3 years, moderate returns (~6-8%).*
Gilt Funds – *Invest in* **government securities** *(safe but interest rate sensitive).*
Credit Risk Funds – *Invest in lower-rated corporate bonds with* **higher returns (~8-10%)** *but more risk.*

Example: *If a retiree wants a steady income, a Debt Fund with SWP (Systematic Withdrawal Plan) can provide monthly returns like a pension.*

3. Hybrid Mutual Funds (Balanced Risk & Return)

Hybrid funds invest in both stocks and bonds, providing a mix of growth and stability.

Types of Hybrid Funds:
Aggressive Hybrid Funds – 65-80% in **stocks**, rest in bonds. **Moderate risk, high return.**
Conservative Hybrid Funds – 70-80% in **bonds**, rest in stocks. *Suitable for low-risk investors.*

Example: *Investors aged* **40-50** *may prefer* **Hybrid Funds** *to balance* **growth & stability***.*

2.2 Classification Based on Investment Style

Active Funds – *Managed by fund managers aiming to* **beat the market.** *Higher expense ratio.*
Passive Funds (Index Funds & ETFs) – *Simply track an index (NIFTY 50, S&P 500). Low-cost & consistent* **returns***.*

Example: *Warren Buffett recommends Index Funds as the safest bet for long-term wealth.*

2.3 Rich Dad Poor Dad Lesson: The Power of Asset Allocation

In Rich Dad Poor Dad, Robert Kiyosaki emphasizes owning assets that generate cash flow.

Mutual funds help by providing multiple asset classes in one portfolio.

Example: *A smart investor doesn't put all money in stocks but diversifies into Equity, Debt, and Hybrid Funds for risk management.*

THREE
HOW MUTUAL FUNDS WORK

*Mutual funds operate by **pooling money** from multiple investors and investing it in a portfolio of assets, managed by professional fund managers. Let's break down the process step by step.*

3.1 The Structure of a Mutual Fund

A mutual fund consists of the following key players:

***Investor** – You, the person investing money in the fund.*

***Asset Management Company (AMC)** – The company managing the mutual fund (e.g., SBI Mutual Fund, HDFC Mutual Fund).*
***Fund Manager** – The expert who makes investment decisions on behalf of investors.*
***Securities and Exchange Board of India (SEBI)** – The regulatory body that ensures mutual funds operate fairly.*
***Custodian & Registrar** – Entities that handle fund operations*

and investor records.

Example: *If you invest in a mutual fund, the fund manager decides how to allocate your money among stocks, bonds, and other assets to generate returns.*

3.2 How Your Investment Grows

You Invest Money → *You buy* **units** *of the mutual fund.* **Fund Manager Allocates Assets** → *Money is invested in* **stocks, bonds, etc.**
Value of Fund Changes Daily → *Based on market performance.*
You Earn Returns → *Through* **capital appreciation** *or* **dividends.**

Example: *If you invest* ₹10,000 *in a mutual fund with a* **Net Asset Value (NAV) of** ₹**100,** *you get* **100 units.** *If the NAV rises to* ₹**120,** *your investment is now worth* ₹12,000!

3.3 Understanding Net Asset Value (NAV)

The **Net Asset Value (NAV)** *represents the* **per-unit price** *of a mutual fund.*

Example: *If a fund has* ₹**1,00,00,000 in assets** *and* **10,00,000 units issued,** *the NAV is* ₹**100 per unit.**

NAV is updated daily based on market performance.

3.4 Systematic Investment Plan (SIP) vs. Lump Sum Investment

SIP (Systematic Investment Plan) – Investing a **fixed amount every month**. Reduces market risk.
Lump Sum Investment – Investing a **large amount at once**. Higher risk, but can yield high returns.

Example: If you invest ₹5,000 per month in an SIP for 20 years at 12% annual returns, you can build a corpus of ₹50+ lakhs!

3.5 Rich Dad Poor Dad Lesson: Let Money Work for You

In Rich Dad Poor Dad, Robert Kiyosaki talks about building assets that generate income. Mutual funds help investors earn passive income through:

1. Dividends from equity funds
2. Interest from debt funds
3. Long-term capital appreciation

Example: Instead of saving ₹1 lakh in a bank, investing in a mutual fund can turn it into ₹15-16 lakhs over 20 years due to compounding.

FOUR

HOW TO INVEST IN MUTUAL FUNDS

*Investing in mutual funds is simple, but choosing the right fund requires a **clear strategy**. This chapter will guide you through the step-by-step process of selecting, investing, and managing mutual funds effectively.*

4.1 Steps to Start Investing in Mutual Funds

Step 1: Define Your Financial Goals

Before investing, identify your goals:

Short-term (1-3 years) – *Buying a car, vacation, emergency fund.*
Medium-term (3-7 years) – *Home down payment, children's education.*
Long-term (7+ years) – *Retirement, wealth creation.*

__Example:__ If you're saving for a car in 2 years, a debt fund is safer. If you want ₹1 crore for retirement in 20 years, go for an equity fund with SIP.

Step 2: Assess Your Risk Appetite

Risk tolerance depends on age, income, and financial security:

__High Risk:__ Young investors with long investment horizons (Invest in equity funds).
__Moderate Risk:__ Middle-aged investors balancing growth & safety (Hybrid funds).
__Low Risk:__ Retirees looking for steady returns (Debt funds).

__Example:__ A 25-year-old investor can take high risks in small-cap funds, while a 50-year-old investor should focus on balanced hybrid funds.

Step 3: Choose the Right Mutual Fund

Types of mutual funds based on risk and return:

__Equity Funds__ – High risk, high return. Best for long-term goals.
__Debt Funds__ – Low risk, stable returns. Ideal for short-term goals.
__Hybrid Funds__ – Balanced risk, moderate returns.

Example: *If your goal is wealth creation, opt for a multi-cap fund with a 10+ year horizon.*

Step 4: Select the Investment Mode

Systematic Investment Plan (SIP) – *Invest a fixed amount monthly, benefiting from* **rupee cost averaging**.
Lump Sum Investment – *Invest a large amount at once, suitable for market dips.*

Example: *Investing* **₹5,000 per month in SIP** *for 15 years at* **12% annual returns** *can grow into* **₹50+ lakhs**!

Step 5: Complete KYC & Open an Account

To invest, complete Know Your Customer (KYC):

PAN Card
Aadhaar Card
Bank Account Details
Email & Mobile Number

Platforms to Invest:
Direct via Mutual Fund Companies (HDFC, ICICI, SBI).
Through Apps/Websites (Groww, Zerodha, Paytm Money).
Banks & Financial Advisors.

4.2 Managing & Monitoring Investments

Check Performance Regularly – Track NAV and fund performance.
Review Portfolio Every 6-12 Months – Rebalance based on market changes.
Reinvest Dividends for Growth – opt for growth plans to maximize compounding.

Note: If an **equity fund underperforms for 3+ years**, consider switching to a better-performing one.

4.3 Rich Dad Poor Dad Lesson: Make Money Work for You

In Rich Dad Poor Dad, Robert Kiyosaki teaches that wealthy people invest in assets rather than saving money. Mutual funds act as an asset that grows over time.

Example: Instead of keeping ₹10 lakh in a savings account, investing it in a mutual fund with 12% returns could grow it to ₹3.5 crore in 30 years.

FIVE

Mutual Fund Performance Metrics

*Investing in mutual funds requires an understanding of key performance metrics. These metrics help investors evaluate **returns, risks, and efficiency** before selecting a fund.*

5.1 Net Asset Value (NAV)

Definition: *The price of one unit of a mutual fund.*

Example: *If a mutual fund has assets worth ₹10 crore and 1 lakh units, the NAV is ₹100 per unit.*

Why it matters:
Helps track fund performance over time.

*Lower NAV does **not** mean a cheaper fund—returns matter more.*

5.2 Expense Ratio

Definition: *The percentage of a fund's total assets deducted for expenses (fund management, admin fees, etc.).*

Example: *If a fund has ₹500 crore in assets and annual expenses of ₹5 crore, the expense ratio is **1%**.*

Why it matters:
Lower expense ratios lead to higher returns over time.
Direct plans have lower expense ratios than regular plans.

5.3 Sharpe Ratio

Definition: *Measures a fund's return relative to its risk. A higher Sharpe Ratio is better.*

Why it matters:
***Higher Sharpe Ratio** means better risk-adjusted returns.*

5.4 Alpha & Beta

Alpha (α) – Fund Manager's Skill

Definition: Measures excess returns a fund generates compared to its benchmark.
Positive Alpha = Fund Outperforms

Negative Alpha = Fund Underperforms.

Example: If an equity fund gives **15% returns**, while the Nifty 50 gives **12%**, Alpha is **+3%**.

Beta (β) – Fund's Volatility

Definition: Measures a fund's **sensitivity to market movements**.

Beta > 1 – More volatile than the market.
Beta < 1 – Less volatile than the market.
Beta = 1 – Moves in line with the market.

Example: A mutual fund with **Beta = 1.2** means **if Nifty 50 moves 10%, the fund moves 12%**.

5.5 Standard Deviation

Definition: *Measures how much a fund's returns* **fluctuate.**
Higher Standard Deviation = More risk and volatility.

Example: *If a fund's average return is 12%, but fluctuates between +18% and -6%, it has a high standard deviation.*

Investors with low risk appetite should prefer funds with lower standard deviation.

5.6 Portfolio Turnover Ratio

Definition: *Shows how frequently a fund buys and sells stocks.*
Higher turnover = More trading = Higher costs.

Example: *If a fund replaces* **80% of its portfolio** *in a year, its turnover ratio is* **80%.**

Long-term investors should prefer funds with lower turnover.

5.7 Rich Dad Poor Dad Lesson: Focus on Asset Efficiency

In Rich Dad Poor Dad, Robert Kiyosaki emphasizes the importance of asset efficiency. High returns do not always mean good investments—risk-adjusted performance matters.

Example: *Instead of chasing high-return, high-risk stocks, a mutual fund investor should check Sharpe Ratio and Alpha before investing*

SIX
MUTUAL FUND REGULATIONS AND TAXATION

*Mutual funds are regulated by financial authorities to protect investors and ensure transparency. Additionally, taxation rules impact the returns on mutual fund investments. This chapter covers **regulations, key governing bodies, and taxation aspects** of mutual funds.*

6.1 Regulatory Bodies Governing Mutual Funds

1. Securities and Exchange Board of India (SEBI)

SEBI *is the main regulator of mutual funds in India.*
It ensures fair practices, investor protection, and transparency.
SEBI sets rules on fund structure, disclosures, expense ratios, and risk management.

Example: SEBI *mandates that mutual fund houses disclose* **Total Expense Ratio (TER)** *and* **risk levels** *of funds.*

2. Association of Mutual Funds in India (AMFI)

AMFI is a self-regulatory organization for mutual fund companies.
It educates investors and promotes ethical fund management.
AMFI issues the ARN (AMFI Registration Number) to mutual fund distributors.

Example: AMFI *introduced the Mutual Fund Sahi Hai campaign to promote awareness.*

3. Reserve Bank of India (RBI) and Government Regulations

RBI monitors banking and financial stability, *ensuring mutual fund investments don't pose risks to the economy.*
The government sets taxation policies and rules on mutual fund investments.

Example: RBI regulates mutual fund investments in foreign assets.

6.2 Taxation of Mutual Funds in India

The tax on mutual funds depends on:
Type of mutual fund (Equity or Debt)
Holding period (Short-term or Long-term)

6.2.1 Tax on Equity Mutual Funds

Short-Term Capital Gains (STCG) – *If units are sold within* **1 year, tax = 15%.**
Long-Term Capital Gains (LTCG) – *If units are sold* **after 1 year, tax = 10% on gains above ₹1 lakh.**

Example: *If you earn ₹1.5 lakh in equity fund profits, ₹50,000 is taxable at 10%.*

6.2.2 Tax on Debt Mutual Funds

Short-Term Capital Gains (STCG) – *Taxed as per the investor's* **income tax slab** *if held for* **less than 3 years.**
Long-Term Capital Gains (LTCG) – 20% tax *with* **indexation benefits** *if held* **for more than 3 years.**

Example: *If a debt fund earns ₹1 lakh in 4 years, after indexation, tax is only ₹5,000 instead of ₹20,000.*

6.2.3 Tax on Hybrid (Balanced) Mutual Funds

Equity-Oriented Hybrid Funds – *Taxed like* **equity funds.**
Debt-Oriented Hybrid Funds – *Taxed like* **debt funds.**

6.3 Dividend Taxation on Mutual Funds

Before 2020 – Dividend was tax-free for investors; fund houses paid **Dividend Distribution Tax (DDT)**.
After 2020 – Dividends are now taxed as **per the investor's income tax slab**.

Example: If an investor in the **30% tax bracket** receives ₹ **50,000 in dividends**, they pay **₹15,000 tax**.

6.4 Tax-Saving Mutual Funds (ELSS)

Equity Linked Savings Scheme (ELSS) offers **tax benefits under Section 80C**.
Investments up to ₹**1.5 lakh per year** are **tax-exempt**.
ELSS has a **3-year lock-in period**, but **highest returns among tax-saving instruments**.

Example: If you invest ₹**1.5 lakh in ELSS**, you save **₹46,800 in taxes** (if in the 30% tax bracket).

6.5 Tax Planning Strategies for Mutual Funds

Hold investments longer to qualify for LTCG tax benefits.
Use ELSS funds to reduce taxable income.
Reinvest dividends to avoid tax burden.
Consider tax-free investment options like PPF and NPS along with mutual funds.

6.6 Rich Dad Poor Dad Lesson: Understanding Taxes on Investments

In Rich Dad Poor Dad, **Robert Kiyosaki** emphasizes that **rich people use tax laws to their advantage.** Investors who **understand taxation** can legally save money and **grow wealth faster.**

Example: Instead of paying 30% tax on fixed deposit interest, an investor can invest in ELSS and debt funds with indexation benefits to reduce tax liability.

SEVEN

RISKS ASSOCIATED WITH MUTUAL FUNDS

*Mutual funds offer **diversification and professional management**, but they are not risk-free. Understanding the **various types of risks** can help investors make better decisions and minimize losses.*

7.1 Types of Risks in Mutual Fund Investments

1. Market Risk (Systematic Risk)

The risk of loss due to overall market fluctuations.
Affected by economic downturns, geopolitical events, inflation, and interest rates.

***Example**: In 2008, the global financial crisis led to a 30-40% decline in stock markets, impacting equity mutual funds.*

How to Reduce It?
Invest for the long term.

Diversify across asset classes (equity, debt, gold).

2. Credit Risk (Default Risk)

Risk that a bond issuer in **debt mutual funds** *may* **fail to repay**.
More common in **low-rated corporate bonds**.

Example: *In 2019,* **IL&FS defaulted**, *causing losses in debt mutual funds that held its bonds.*

How to Reduce It?
Choose funds investing in AAA-rated bonds.
Check the credit rating of the fund's portfolio.

3. Interest Rate Risk

Changes in interest rates impact bond prices, affecting debt mutual funds.
If interest rates rise, bond prices fall, leading to losses.

Example: *In 2022, the US Federal Reserve hiked interest rates, reducing debt fund returns worldwide.*

How to Reduce It?
Invest in short-duration debt funds if rates are rising.
Hold long-term bonds when rates are expected to fall.

4. Liquidity Risk

Risk of not being able to sell fund units easily.
More common in small-cap, sectoral, and closed-ended funds.

Example: *During the COVID-19 crash in 2020, some debt funds faced redemption pressure, leading to losses.*

How to Reduce It?
*Invest in **open-ended mutual funds** for easy withdrawals.*
Avoid sectoral funds with low trading volumes.

5. Inflation Risk

If inflation rises faster than investment returns, real purchasing power declines.
Affects fixed-income investments and low-return funds.

Example: *If inflation is **7%** but your **debt fund returns 6%**, your **real return is negative**.*

How to Reduce It?
*Invest in **equity funds**, which historically outpace inflation.*
*Use **gold and real estate funds** as inflation hedges.*

6. Concentration Risk

Risk of investing too much in **one stock, sector, or asset class**. If that sector underperforms, the entire portfolio suffers.

Example: Tech-focused mutual funds dropped sharply in **2022** when global tech stocks crashed.

How to Reduce It?
Diversify across **sectors, geographies, and asset classes**. Avoid **overexposure** to any single investment.

7. Regulatory Risk

Changes in government policies and SEBI regulations can impact mutual funds.
Tax changes, investment restrictions, or compliance rules can affect returns.

Example: In 2023, SEBI revised **expense ratio rules**, reducing profits for mutual fund companies.

How to Reduce It?
Stay updated on regulatory changes.
Choose funds that comply with SEBI norms.

7.2 Rich Dad Poor Dad Lesson: Risk vs. Control

In Rich Dad Poor Dad, **Robert Kiyosaki** explains that wealthy investors control their risks. He emphasizes that lack of knowledge, not investment itself, is risky.

Example: *A rich investor studies* **market cycles and risk factors** *before investing, while a poor investor follows* **blind advice** *and suffers losses.*

• 29 •

Lesson:
Knowledge reduces risk—*learn before investing.*
Control your investments—*diversify and track market trends.*

7.3 How to Manage Mutual Fund Risks?

Diversify your portfolio—*invest across asset classes.*
Use SIPs (Systematic Investment Plans)—*reduce the impact of market volatility.*
Check fund ratings and past performance *before investing.*
Rebalance your portfolio regularly *to align with financial goals.*

EIGHT

STRATEGIES FOR MAXIMIZING RETURNS

*Investing in mutual funds is not just about **choosing the right fund**—it's about using **strategies** to maximize returns. This chapter explores proven approaches that can help investors grow their wealth efficiently.*

8.1 The Power of Asset Allocation

What is Asset Allocation?
*Asset allocation is distributing investments across **equities, debt, gold, and other assets** to balance risk and return.*

Example:

*A **young investor** (age 25) may invest **80% in equity funds** and **20% in debt funds** for growth.*

A **retired investor** (age 60) may invest **70% in debt funds** and **30% in equity** for stability.

Best Practices:
Adjust allocation based on **age, goals, and risk tolerance.**
Review and rebalance **every 6-12 months.**

8.2 Diversification: Don't Put All Eggs in One Basket

What is Diversification?
It means investing in **multiple sectors, asset classes, and geographies** to reduce risk.

Example:

A portfolio with **only tech stocks** dropped sharply in 2022 when tech stocks crashed.

A **diversified portfolio** with equity, debt, and international funds reduced losses.

Best Practices:
Invest in **different mutual fund categories** (equity, debt, hybrid, gold, etc.).
Consider **international funds** for global exposure.

8.3 Systematic Investment Plan (SIP): The Power of Compounding

What is SIP?

SIP allows investors to invest **a fixed amount regularly** in mutual funds, benefiting from **rupee cost averaging** and **compounding**.

Example:

- Investing ₹10,000/month for 20 years at 12% returns = ₹ 1 crore+

- Investing ₹10,000/month for 30 years at 12% returns = ₹ 3.5 crore+

Best Practices:
Start SIP **early** and **increase SIP amounts** yearly.
Continue SIPs during **market downturns** for higher returns.

8.4 Systematic Transfer Plan (STP) for Smart Investing

What is STP?
STP helps **shift money gradually** from a debt fund to an equity fund.

Example: If you have ₹5 lakh in a liquid fund, you can **transfer ₹25,000 per month** into an equity fund instead of investing in one lump sum.

Best Practices:
*Use STP when moving from **low-risk debt funds to equity funds**.*
*Useful when investing **lump sum amounts** after a windfall.*

8.5 Systematic Withdrawal Plan (SWP) for Regular Income

What is SWP?
*SWP allows investors to **withdraw a fixed amount** monthly from mutual funds, ensuring **steady income**.*

Example:

- *A retiree with ₹**50 lakh in a mutual fund** can withdraw ₹30,000/month using SWP while keeping the capital invested.*

Best Practices:
*Use SWP in **debt funds** for stability.*
*Ideal for **retirement planning**.*

8.6 Tactical vs. Strategic Investing

Strategic Investing (Long-term Focus)

-

*Invest in a **d**iversified portfolio and hold for 5-10+ years.*

.

Focus on consistent SIPs and goal-based investing.

• 34 •

Tactical Investing (Short-term Adjustments)

.

Adjust portfolio based on market trends and economic conditions.

.

Example: Increasing gold investment when inflation rises.

Best Practices:
*Stick to strategic investing for **long-term wealth creation**.*
*Use tactical investing **cautiously** and avoid frequent changes.*

8.7 Rich Dad Poor Dad Lesson: The Difference Between Investors and Speculators

*In Rich Dad Poor Dad, **Robert Kiyosaki** highlights how **rich investors** focus on **long-term strategies**, while **poor investors chase quick profits**.*

Example:

rich investor follows asset allocation, diversification, and SIPs to grow wealth steadily.

A poor investor buys funds based on hot trends and exits in panic, losing money.

Lesson:
Think long-term, *not short-term profits.*
Follow a disciplined approach *to investing.*

8.8 Key Takeaways for Maximizing Mutual Fund Returns

Start investing early *to benefit from compounding.*
Choose the right asset allocation *based on age and goals.*
Use SIP, STP, and SWP strategies *for smart investing.*
Avoid emotional decisions—*stick to long-term plans.*

NINE

How to Choose the Right Mutual Fund

*Choosing the right mutual fund is a crucial step toward building long-term wealth. With thousands of funds available, investors must evaluate them based on **performance, risk, cost, and suitability** for their financial goals.*

*This chapter provides a **step-by-step guide** to selecting the best mutual fund.*

9.1 Define Your Investment Goals

Why is Goal-Based Investing Important?
Investors should align their mutual fund selection with their financial goals.

Examples of Investment Goals:

.

Short-term (1-3 years): *Buying a car, vacation, emergency fund →* **Debt funds**

Medium-term (3-7 years): *Down payment for a house, child's education →* **Hybrid/Balanced funds**

Long-term (7+ years): *Retirement, wealth creation →* **Equity funds**

Best Practices:
Always **define a clear goal** *before investing.*
Choose funds that match **time horizon and risk appetite.**

9.2 Understanding Risk Appetite

What is Risk Appetite?
Risk appetite is the **ability to tolerate losses** *in pursuit of higher returns.*

Investor Profiles & Suitable Funds:

Aggressive (High Risk Tolerance): *Invests in* **Small-cap, Mid-cap, Thematic Funds**

Moderate (Medium Risk Tolerance): *Invests in* **Large-cap, Hybrid Funds**

Conservative (Low Risk Tolerance): *Prefers **Debt Funds, Liquid Funds***

Best Practices:
Identify your risk profile before investing.
Use a risk assessment questionnaire provided by AMCs.

9.3 Evaluating Fund Performance

How to Assess Fund Performance?
A fund's historical returns give insights into its consistency.

Key Performance Metrics:

Annualized Returns: *1-year, 3-year, 5-year, 10-year performance.*

Benchmark Comparison: *Check if the fund **beats its index** (Nifty 50, S&P BSE Sensex, etc.).*

Rolling Returns: *Consistency of performance across different market cycles.*

Best Practices:
Choose funds with consistent performance over 5-10 years.
Avoid funds with extreme fluctuations in returns.

9.4 Expense Ratio & Cost Analysis

What is Expense Ratio?
The expense ratio is the annual fee charged by the fund house for managing your investment.

Expense Ratio Impact:

If two funds give the same returns, the one with lower expense ratio is better.

Actively managed funds have a higher expense ratio than Index Funds & ETFs.

Best Practices:
Choose low-cost funds with good performance.
Compare Direct Plans vs. Regular Plans (Direct plans have lower expense ratios).

9.5 Fund Manager's Track Record

Why Does the Fund Manager Matter?
*A skilled fund manager can **make better investment decisions** in changing market conditions.*

How to Evaluate a Fund Manager?

Experience in handling market crashes and recoveries.

Past performance across multiple funds.

Consistency in investment philosophy.

Best Practices:
Prefer funds managed by experienced professionals with a solid track record.

9.6 How to Read a Mutual Fund Fact Sheet?

What is a Mutual Fund Fact Sheet?
*A fact sheet is a **report** that provides key details about a mutual fund.*

Key Sections to Check:

Fund Objective: *Purpose of the fund (growth, income, stability).*

Top Holdings: *Stocks/bonds the fund has invested in.*

Risk Level: *Indicates **low, medium, or high risk**.*

Expense Ratio & NAV: *Costs and current value of the fund.*

Best Practices:
*Read the fact sheet **before investing** in any fund.*
*Compare **two or more funds** before making a decision.*

9.7 Rich Dad Poor Dad Lesson: Making Smart Investment Choices

In Rich Dad Poor Dad, **Robert Kiyosaki** *emphasizes the* **importance of financial education** *in investment decisions.*

Example: **Poor Dad** *blindly invested in* **mutual funds suggested by agents**. **Rich Dad** *researched funds, studied financial statements, and* **made informed choices**.

Lesson: *Educate yourself before investing. Don't follow the herd—analyze funds based on research.*

9.8 Checklist for Selecting a Mutual Fund

Define financial goals and time horizon.
Assess risk tolerance.
Compare historical performance of funds.
Check expense ratio and fund manager's track record.
Read the fund fact sheet carefully.

TEN

SELECTING A MUTUAL FUND BASED ON AGE

*Choosing the right mutual fund depends on **age, financial goals, and risk tolerance.** This chapter provides a structured approach to selecting mutual funds based on different life stages.*

10.1 Why Age Matters in Investment Decisions

Age is a key factor in risk tolerance and financial goals. Young investors can take higher risks for higher returns. Older investors need capital protection and stability.

Example:

A 25-year-old investor can invest more in equity funds.

A 60-year-old retiree needs low-risk debt funds and income-generating schemes.

Best Practices:
Align investments with life stage and financial goals.
Adjust portfolio allocation as you age.

10.2 Investment Strategy for Different Age Groups

1. Age 20-30: High-Growth Strategy

Investment Objective: Wealth creation, long-term growth.
Risk Tolerance: High.

Suggested Mutual Funds:
Equity Funds (Small-cap, Mid-cap, Large-cap) → High return potential.
Index Funds & ETFs → Low-cost passive investing.
Sectoral/Thematic Funds → Tech, Pharma, or Global markets.
SIP (Systematic Investment Plan) → For long-term wealth building.

Pro Tip:

- Start investing **early** to benefit from **compounding**.

- Invest **at least 70% in equity funds** for aggressive growth.

2. Age 30-40: Balanced Growth & Stability

Investment Objective: Wealth accumulation, home purchase, child's education.
Risk Tolerance: Moderate to High.

Suggested Mutual Funds:
Large & Mid-Cap Equity Funds → Balanced risk-return.
Balanced Hybrid Funds → Mix of equity and debt.
Debt Funds (Short-term, Liquid Funds) → Emergency funds.
ELSS (Equity-Linked Savings Scheme) → Tax-saving investment.

Pro Tip:

Maintain **60-70% in equities, 30-40% in debt** for stability.

Increase **SIP amounts** with salary hikes.

3. Age 40-50: Risk Mitigation & Stability

Investment Objective: Capital protection, child's higher education, early retirement planning.
Risk Tolerance: Moderate.

Suggested Mutual Funds:
Large-cap Equity Funds → Stability & growth.
Debt-Oriented Hybrid Funds → Lower volatility.

Gold ETFs & Index Funds → *Inflation hedge.*
Short-Term Debt Funds → *Low-risk, steady returns.*

Pro Tip:

Reduce equity exposure to **40-50%**.

Increase allocation to **debt funds & hybrid funds**.

4. Age 50-60: Capital Protection & Income Focus

Investment Objective: *Retirement corpus, steady income.*
Risk Tolerance: *Low to Moderate.*

Suggested Mutual Funds:
Debt Mutual Funds (Gilt, Short-term, Liquid Funds) → *Low risk.*
Dividend-Paying Balanced Funds → *Monthly/quarterly income.*
Hybrid Funds (Debt-Heavy) → *Stability with moderate growth.*
Post Office Monthly Income Scheme (POMIS) → *Safe income option.*

Pro Tip:

Allocate **30-40% to equities, 60-70% to debt instruments**.

*Focus on **regular income generation.***

5. Age 60 & Beyond: Capital Preservation & Regular Income

Investment Objective: *Financial security, wealth preservation, and stable income.*
Risk Tolerance: *Low.*

Suggested Mutual Funds:
Senior Citizen Saving Schemes (SCSS) → *Government-backed safety.*
Debt Mutual Funds (Liquid, Ultra-Short-term, Gilt Funds) → *Low risk.*
Fixed Deposits (FDs) & SWP (Systematic Withdrawal Plan) → *Regular cash flow.*
Government Bonds & Annuities → *Safe and predictable returns.*

Pro Tip:

Minimize equity exposure *(<20%) to protect capital.*

Use **Systematic Withdrawal Plan (SWP)** *for a steady income.*

10.3 Case Study: Rich Dad vs. Poor Dad's Investment Approach

In Rich Dad Poor Dad, **Robert Kiyosaki** emphasizes the importance of **financial education** in investment decisions.

Example: Poor Dad invested in low-yield savings & fixed deposits → Safe but low returns. Rich Dad strategically diversified in stocks, real estate, and mutual funds → High wealth creation.

Lesson:
Invest wisely based on **age and financial goals**.
Diversify your portfolio instead of relying on low-yield savings.

10.4 Final Thoughts

Key Takeaways:
Young investors should focus on growth-oriented equity funds.
Mid-life investors should balance equity & debt.
Older investors should focus on capital protection & regular income.

Action Steps:
Reassess your portfolio every 5-10 years.
Adjust mutual fund allocation as per age and financial goals.

ELEVEN

THE FUTURE OF MUTUAL FUNDS

*Mutual funds are continuously evolving with **technological advancements, regulatory changes, and shifting investor preferences**. This chapter explores the key trends that will shape the future of the mutual fund industry.*

11.1 The Role of Technology in Mutual Funds

Key Innovations Transforming Mutual Funds:
Artificial Intelligence (AI) & Machine Learning (ML) *– AI-driven portfolio management and risk assessment.*
Robo-Advisors *– Automated investment services offering personalized fund recommendations.*
Blockchain & Smart Contracts *– Enhancing security, transparency, and efficiency in fund transactions.*
Big Data Analytics *– Predictive insights for better investment decisions.*
Mobile & Digital Platforms *– Easy access to mutual fund investments with apps and AI-powered assistants.*

Case Study: Rich Dad's View on Innovation
In Rich Dad Poor Dad, **Robert Kiyosaki** emphasizes staying ahead of the curve.

Poor Dad resisted new financial tools and lost investment opportunities.

Rich Dad embraced innovation, using **data-driven decisions** to build wealth.

Lesson: Investors who adapt to technological advancements will gain better returns.

11.2 Passive Investing & the Rise of Index Funds

Active funds are losing popularity due to higher fees & underperformance.
Index Funds & Exchange-Traded Funds (ETFs) are gaining traction.

Future Trends:
Low-cost index investing will dominate the market.
More investors will shift from actively managed funds to passive funds.
Fund managers will adopt hybrid active-passive strategies.

Example: Warren Buffett recommends index funds for long-term investors due to low costs & stable returns.

11.3 Growth of ESG & Sustainable Investing

What is ESG Investing?
ESG stands for **Environmental, Social, and Governance.**
Investors prefer funds that focus on:
Environmental impact – Companies reducing carbon footprints.
Social responsibility – Ethical labor practices.
Good governance – Transparency and compliance.

Future Outlook:
ESG Funds will grow due to global sustainability concerns.
Governments may offer **tax benefits** for ESG investments.
Investors will demand **higher corporate accountability**.

Case Study: Tesla & ESG Funds

Tesla is a top pick in ESG funds due to its sustainable business model. More investors are choosing green energy & sustainable investments.

Lesson: Investing in ESG mutual funds can align with both **profit and purpose.**

11.4 Personalized & Goal-Based Investing

Investors are moving from generic funds to customized portfolios.
Mutual funds will offer personalized goal-based solutions.

Upcoming Features:
AI-powered fund selection based on financial goals.
More options for thematic investing (Technology, Healthcare, Green Energy).
Increased use of algorithm-driven financial planning.

11.5 Globalization & Cross-Border Investing

Key Trends in Global Investing:
*Mutual funds will offer **global exposure** in emerging markets. International Funds will become **more accessible** for retail investors.*
*Investors will diversify beyond domestic markets to **reduce risk**.*

Example: Indian Investors in the US Market

Many Indian investors are investing in Nasdaq 100 & S&P 500 funds for higher returns. International mutual funds allow diversification across global economies.

Lesson: *Investing in global markets reduces risk & enhances returns.*

11.6 Regulatory Changes & Investor Protection

What's Changing?
Stronger SEBI regulations to protect retail investors.
Mutual funds must ensure more transparency in fee structures.
Use of real-time data monitoring to prevent fraud.

Example: SEBI's Role in Investor Protection

SEBI has introduced strict disclosure norms to improve mutual fund transparency.

Lesson: Future investors will benefit from **safer & more regulated** mutual funds.

11.7 The Future of SIPs & Digital Investing

Key Developments:
SIPs will become more flexible, allowing investors to adjust contributions easily.
Mutual fund apps will integrate AI & voice assistants for easy investing.
Micro-investing (starting with ₹100) will make mutual funds more accessible.

Example: Rise of Digital SIPs

Young investors are using apps like Zerodha Coin, Groww, Paytm Money to automate SIPs.

Lesson: *The future of mutual funds is **digital, accessible, and automated.***

11.8 Final Thoughts on the Future of Mutual Funds

Key Takeaways:
Technology will drive the mutual fund industry (AI, blockchain, big data).
ESG funds & passive investing will gain popularity.
Global investing & personalized funds will become mainstream.
Regulations will enhance investor protection.

Action Steps for Investors:
Stay updated with new trends & emerging technologies.
Diversify investments across asset classes & geographies.
Adapt to new investment strategies & digital platforms.

TWELVE

COMMON SHORT FORMS AND THEIR MEANINGS IN PORTFOLIO STUDY

Understanding financial jargon and abbreviations is essential for studying mutual funds and building an investment portfolio. This chapter covers commonly used short forms, their meanings, and their relevance in mutual fund investments.

General Investment Terms

AUM – Assets Under Management: The total market value of investments managed by a mutual fund or financial institution.

NAV – Net Asset Value: The per-unit value of a mutual fund, calculated daily.

ETF – Exchange-Traded Fund: A fund traded like a stock, tracking an index or sector.

FoF – Fund of Funds: A mutual fund that invests in other mutual funds.

SIP – Systematic Investment Plan: A method of investing fixed amounts regularly in mutual funds.

STP – Systematic Transfer Plan: A strategy to transfer money from one mutual fund to another systematically.

SWP – Systematic Withdrawal Plan: A method of withdrawing fixed amounts from a mutual fund investment regularly.

Risk and Performance Metrics

CAGR – Compound Annual Growth Rate: Measures an investment's average annual growth over time.

XIRR – Extended Internal Rate of Return: Used for SIPs to calculate real returns.

SD – Standard Deviation: Indicates volatility in a mutual fund's returns.

Beta – Measures a fund's sensitivity to market movements. A beta of 1 means the fund moves in sync with the market.

Alpha – Measures a fund's performance compared to its benchmark. Positive alpha indicates outperformance.

Sharpe Ratio – Measures risk-adjusted returns. A higher ratio suggests better risk-adjusted performance.

Sortino Ratio – Similar to the Sharpe ratio but only considers downside risk.

Taxation and Regulatory Terms

STCG – Short-Term Capital Gains: Tax on profits from selling mutual fund units within a short period.

LTCG – Long-Term Capital Gains: Tax on profits from long-term mutual fund holdings.

DDT – Dividend Distribution Tax: Previously applicable tax on dividends, now taxed in the hands of investors.

ELSS – Equity-Linked Savings Scheme: A tax-saving mutual fund under Section 80C.

AMFI – Association of Mutual Funds in India: A self-regulatory organization for the mutual fund industry.

SEBI – Securities and Exchange Board of India: The regulator of the securities market and mutual funds

THIRTEEN
CASE STUDIES & REAL-LIFE EXAMPLES

*Understanding mutual funds through **real-world case studies** provides valuable insights into **investment strategies, risks, and long-term wealth creation.** This chapter highlights success stories, lessons from market crashes, and insights from Rich Dad Poor Dad.*

12.1 The Power of Systematic Investment Plans (SIPs)

Case Study: Ramesh's 20-Year SIP Journey

Background: In 2002, Ramesh, a 25-year-old engineer, started investing ₹**5,000 per month** in a diversified equity fund through SIP.

Strategy: He **never** stopped investing, even during market crashes (2008 crisis, 2020 COVID crash).

Outcome: By 2022, his investments **grew to ₹1.8 crore**, benefiting from **compounding & market rebounds**.

Lessons Learned:

SIPs **mitigate market volatility** and benefit from **rupee cost averaging**.

Long-term investing in equity mutual funds **outperforms traditional savings**.

12.2 How Market Crashes Create Opportunities

Case Study: 2008 Financial Crisis – Mutual Fund Investors Who Stayed Invested

Scenario: The 2008 financial crisis caused a **50% market crash**, and many investors panicked.

Mistake: Those who **exited the market** suffered losses.

Success Story: Smart investors who **stayed invested & continued SIPs** saw their portfolio **triple** by 2013.

Lessons Learned:

Market crashes are **temporary**; staying invested pays off.

Panic selling leads to real losses, while long-term patience leads to recovery.

Rich Dad's View on Market Crashes

Rich Dad said, "Recessions are the best time to buy assets at a discount."

Poor Dad feared downturns and **missed wealth-building opportunities**.

12.3 The Cost of Delaying Investments

Case Study: Amit vs. Rahul – Early vs. Late Investing

Final Corpus (at 60)

Amit at 25 starts ₹5,000 SIP for 35 Years the final amount will be ₹6.4 Crores

Rahul at 35 starts ₹10,000 SIP for 25 Years the final anount will be ₹3.2 Crores

Lessons Learned:

Starting early is more powerful than investing more later.

Compounding rewards patience—time in the market matters more than timing.

Rich Dad's Advice:

"Make your money work for you as early as possible."

12.4 Choosing the Wrong Mutual Fund: A Costly Mistake

Case Study: Anil's High-Expense Fund Trap

Mistake: Anil invested in a regular mutual fund plan with a 2.5% expense ratio.

Outcome: After 10 years, his returns were ₹8 lakh lower than a direct plan with a 1% expense ratio.

Lessons Learned:

Always check the expense ratio before investing.

Direct plans have lower costs and higher long-term returns.

12.5 Successful Retirement Planning with Mutual Funds

Case Study: Priya's Retirement Corpus with Mutual Funds

Goal: *Priya wanted ₹3 crore for retirement at 60.*

Strategy: *Started investing ₹10,000 per month in hybrid funds & large-cap funds at 30.*

Outcome: *She accumulated ₹3.2 crore by 60 with disciplined investing.*

Lessons Learned:

Hybrid & equity funds provide long-term stability.

Retirement planning should start early for financial independence.

12.6 The Future Investor: Adapting to New Trends

Case Study: Rohit's Investment in International Funds

Scenario: *Rohit diversified his portfolio by investing 30% in US-based index funds.*

Outcome: *While Indian markets fluctuated, his global investments balanced risks.*

Lessons Learned: *Diversification across global markets reduces risks.*

New investors must embrace global trends like ETFs & ESG funds.

Final Takeaways from Case Studies

SIPs & long-term investing create wealth.
Market crashes are opportunities, not threats.
Early investing is more powerful than investing more later.
Low-cost funds outperform high-fee funds.
Global & diversified portfolios reduce risk.

Conclusion

Mutual funds have transformed the way individuals invest, making wealth creation accessible to everyone. Whether you are a beginner looking to start small or an experienced investor planning for retirement, mutual funds offer a flexible and diversified way to grow your money.

Key Takeaways from This Book

Understanding Mutual Funds: *Mutual funds pool money from investors and offer professionally managed portfolios.*
Choosing the Right Fund: *Different types of funds suit different risk appetites and financial goals.*
Investing Wisely: *SIPs help navigate market fluctuations, while lump-sum investments work in strong markets.*
Avoiding Common Mistakes: *High expense ratios, emotional decisions, and lack of diversification can hurt returns.*
The Power of Time: *Early investing leads to exponential growth due to compounding.*
Risk & Reward Balance: *Diversification and periodic rebalancing can protect your investments.*

Final Thought: The Rich Dad Perspective

In Rich Dad Poor Dad, Robert Kiyosaki emphasizes:
"The poor work for money. The rich make money work for them."

This applies perfectly to mutual fund investing. By consistently investing, staying patient, and making informed financial decisions, you allow your money to work for you. The secret to wealth-building isn't just how much you invest, but how long you stay invested.

Your Next Steps

Start investing today—even small amounts grow over time.
Choose funds wisely based on your age, goals, and risk tolerance.
Stay invested for the long term and avoid emotional decisions.
Keep learning—financial knowledge is key to smart investing.